SH!T
JOKES

By Joe King

Scarlet
Editions

For Barn Dog and Penny Poo Poo

CONTENTS

3

SPOUSE SHiT

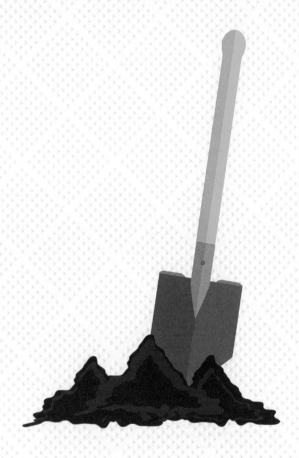

I think I've cured my wife's fear of being buried alive.
The screams stopped about an hour ago.

I recently watched my wedding video backwards.
I love it when I take the ring off her finger,
leave the church and go drinking with my friends.

My wife accused me of having an affair with a girl from
Llanfairpwllgwyngyllgogerychwyrndrobwllllantysiliogogogoch.
How could she say that?

My wife asked me to pass her the lip balm
but I gave her some superglue instead.
She's still not talking to me!

My husband says it was my obsession with horoscopes
that Taurus apart.

Wife: Why do you talk about my weight behind my back?
Husband: By the time I get around to the front,
I've forgotten what I was going to say.

My wife's a terrible cook, she can never get her sauces right!
I've stuck with her though, through thick and thin.

Why did my wife cross the road?
To get back to the first shoe shop we went in three fucking hours ago!

My wife asked me earlier what my plans were for Easter?
"The same as Jesus" I replied.
"Disappear Thursday, turn up Monday!"

SPOUSE SH!T

I bought my husband a power fan for his birthday.
He was blown away.

My wife asked me to bring home some stuff for the pancakes.
She wasn't happy when I came back with a push-up bra.

What do you do if your wife keeps moaning at you?
Put the phone down and order another drink from the bar.

My wife is temperamental.
50% temper,
50% mental.

Even though I've been married for five years
I still can't help thinking about the one that got away.
My wife's ex. What a lucky bastard.

My Mrs has recently started eating sofas...
It's weird... but then again she's always had a suite tooth.

My wife is so ugly she spent five hours in the beauty salon...
just getting a quote.

My Mrs and three of her pals squeezed into my car after weight watchers.
I muttered "Fat cows." The Mrs snapped "What was that!?"
I said "You Herd."

Just noticed the wife is wearing her sexy underwear.
This can only mean one thing.
She's behind with the washing!

My husband is going to a fancy dress party as a Rastafarian
and he's asked me to do his hair.
I'm dreading it.

I met my wife at speed dating.
She was livid.

Why do men die before their wives?
They want to.

Today I looked at my wife and thought.
This is the only investment which has doubled in my lifetime.

Found out recently that my husband had an affair with a midget.
I can't believe he would stoop so low.

The wife said she wanted to go and see Jeremy Kyle Live for her birthday.
So I got her sister pregnant!
We're on next Wednesday!

The wife complains that I don't take any interest in our children.
That's the last time I offer to pick up the fat one from school!

My wife caught me masturbating to an optical illusion.
I told her it's not what it looks like.

My wife is very big in fashion.
She's a size 22.

My wife told me to prepare our ginger son for his first day at school.
So I beat him up and took his dinner money off him.

I always call out my wife's name during sex.
Just to make sure she's not around.

My wife broke up with me recently because I'm a compulsive gambler.
All I can think about is how to win her back.

An Arab offered me forty camels for my wife.
Unfortunately I don't smoke.

Marriage is a relationship where one person is always right
and the other is the husband.

Took the wife's Valentine's present back today.
She said she wanted something black and lacy.
Turns out she didn't mean football boots.

What's the difference between a penis and a bonus?
Your wife will blow your bonus.

The Mrs started her menstrual cycle today and she's bet me that
I can't go a week without making a joke out of it.
I said you're on!

How do I disable the autocorrect function on my wife?

Some mornings I wake up bitchy.
Other mornings I just let her sleep.

I went dogging with the wife last night... never again!
By the time she'd finished parking the car everyone had fucked off!

I still miss my ex-wife...
but my aim is getting better.

I haven't spoken to my wife for 18 months!
I don't like to interrupt her.

Whilst having sex I suddenly stopped and didn't move.
Wife said "What are you doing?"
I said "I've seen this on the internet, it's called buffering."

I absolutely hate my mother-in-law.
She's actually quite a nice person,
but she brought my husband into the world.

"Sir your car was swerving all over the road."
"Sorry officer I've had ten pints and feel pissed."
"That's no excuse to let your wife drive."

I was shopping with the wife for a present for her mother.
She said she wanted something electric.
I suggested a chair.

My wife's parking is unparalleled.

My Mrs has been told she'll have to lose weight if
she wants to become pregnant.
I told her.

I wrote 'DIVORCE', my wife wrote 'YES'.
Tough way to find out, but at least I won our last game of Scrabble.

The good thing about marriage is that
you can have sex at any time you want.
As long as you're the one with the vagina.

I gave blood yesterday.
I know it's not the usual sort of thing you give your wife
on Valentine's Day, but it came from the heart.

I came home to find my wife horny.
"Tie me up and you can do anything you want", she said.
So I tied her up and went golfing.

The wife thinks it's cruel we've started testing our new products on rabbits. She's got a point, I suppose. I work in a hammer factory.

A man gets the words 'I love you' tattooed on his penis. He goes home and shows his wife. His wife says "Don't try to put words in my mouth."

When a man steals your wife, there is no better revenge than to let him keep her.

I said to my wife the other day, "Why don't you tell me when you have an orgasm?" She said "I don't like to ring you when you're at work!"

My wife has old hoover syndrome. She makes a constant whining noise and doesn't suck anymore.

My wife has left me; she says I love football more than I love her. I'm gutted; we've been together for ten seasons!

People often ask me what my Mrs does, but it's difficult to say really. She sells seashells on the seashore.

Sat watching TV when the wife walked past and turned it off. After a few minutes staring at a blank screen. I thought... that's not on!

Maths made simple.
If you have £20 and your wife has £5,
she has £25.

Spent some time at the wife's grave earlier.
Bless her, she thinks I'm digging a pond!

Persuaded my wife to smuggle coke through customs by sticking
it up her arse! Feel pretty bad about it now,
I didn't know you could buy another can in the departure lounge.

The wife was watching a cookery show. I said
"What the fuck you watching that for? You can't cook!"
She said "You watch porn you fat bastard."

I was busy having sex with the wife when I felt a tap on my shoulder.
I hate fucking in the bath.

I bought the Mrs a new bag and a new belt for her birthday.
She'll be made up! The hoover is as good as new now.

My wife is so tired at the end of the day
she can hardly keep her mouth open.

My wife came home with a vibrator, started waving it about screaming,
"I don't need you now, I don't need you now!"
Guess who had to put the batteries in?

Wife: "Did you know, butterflies only live for two days?"
I said, "Honey, I think that's a myth."
She said, "No, it's definitely a butterfly."

I said to my friend "My wife's a peach."
He asked: "Because she's so soft and juicy?"
I replied "No, because she has a heart of stone."

I'm not saying the wife's fat but...
She puts her belt on with a boomerang.

My wife complained that I'm trying to be someone I'm not.
I'm just confused as to how she got into the Batcave.

My wife has left me. She said I was too passive,
and didn't stand up for myself enough.
I can't argue with that.

My wife just left me because of my obsession with cricket.
It's really hit me for 6!

My wife accused me of being a transvestite.
So I packed her things and left!

As it's Valentine's Day the Mrs has said
she'll go on top tonight for a change.
I love our bunk beds!

Our last fight was my fault...
My wife asked, "What's on the TV?"
I said, "Dust!"

My husband and I are having a competition to see who can steal the most dog related stuff from our local pet shop.
I've just taken the lead!

The wife told me to go out and get her something to look nice.
So I came back with a litre of vodka and some lager!

The Mrs is not happy. I replaced our bed with a trampoline.
She hit the roof.

I don't trust anything that bleeds for five days and doesn't die.

"You haven't listened to a word I've said, have you?"
Always seems like a strange way for my wife
to start a conversation with me.

My wife says she's leaving me because of my addiction
to antidepressants.
Won't be needing them anymore then.

I wouldn't say that my wife is fat, but when she walks past the TV
I miss four adverts!

Marriage is like a deck of cards.
In the beginning all you need is two hearts and a diamond.
By the end you wish you had club and a spade.

Wife to husband "Let's go out and have some fun tonight!"
Husband: "Ok, but if you get home before I do,
leave the hall light on."

How can you tell if your wife is dead?
The sex is the same but the dishes pile up!

My wife's fanny smells like roses.
But Rose's fanny is tighter.

The wife's just bought eight venison legs for £30.
I think that's two deer!

I always carry a picture of my wife and children in my wallet.
It reminds me why there's no money in there.

Had a bit of back door action with the wife when I got back
from the pub last night.
She locked me out so I had to kick it in.

My husband left me because he said I'm obsessed with the muppets.
Apparently, I'm not ready for a Kermitment.

Me: When I was younger I was given a choice, a long penis or
a good memory. Wife: Which one did you choose?
Me: I can't remember!

My wife accused me of having OCD.
I soon put her in her place.

My wife is obsessed with her new tropical juice diet.
It's enough to make a mango crazy.

Wife texts husband 'Windows frozen!'
He replies 'Just pour some slightly hot water over it.'
Wife: 'Computer's totally fucked now!'

I went window shopping with the wife earlier today.
I bought four windows.

My wife keeps complaining about my premature ejaculation.
She took it on the chin at first but now it just gets on her tits!

As she was dying, a woman called her husband
and said, "I've been unfaithful." Husband replies,
"I know. That's why I poisoned you."

Wife said we should try some 'role reversal' in bed.
So I said I had a headache.

My wife loves sad movies, and says she can tell how
good it was by how many Kleenex she goes through.
I have the same system.

I'm not saying that my wife is fat,
but I've had to put an energy saving lightbulb in the fridge.

I love Wales, In fact I took the Mrs to Wales a few weeks ago.
To Bangor.

After years of doubt, I'm convinced my wife's having an affair.
We've moved 250 miles away and we've still got the same
fucking window cleaner.

My wife is complaining that I never buy her jewellery.
In my defence, I didn't even know she sold jewellery.

The Mrs says I'm tight, so to prove her wrong
we went out for tea and biscuits, it was quite exciting
as she's never given blood before.

I've just bought a house with period features.
My wife really hates that nickname.

Occasionally I wake up grumpy.
But most of the time I just tip-toe out of the bedroom and leave her.

Son: What does gay mean?
Dad: It means happy.
Son: So are you gay, then?
Dad: No, son, I have a wife.

SPOUSE SH!T

Told my husband that I don't want to go to an 80's fancy dress party.
But he remains adamant.

Why should you always get your wife to buy trousers for you?
Because chinos what's best.

A recent study has found that women who carry a little extra weight
live longer than the men who mention it!

My wife says I'm spoken for.

Since it started raining, all my wife has done is look sadly
through the window...
if it gets any worse, I'll have to let her in.

I thought my wife was happy to fully repair my jeans.
Or at least sew its seams.

My wife has threatened to leave me over my obsession
with 70's American comedy.
Happy days!

My wife said "It'd be nice if one day I came home
from work and the housework was done!"
I said "Well, get up earlier and do it before you go!"

Childbirth is the most painful thing in the world said my wife.
A kick in the bollocks is worse I said,
after one you never want another.

The wife asked me to get that spray that makes the curtains smell nicer.
I bought her some femfresh.

Me and the Mrs bought a waterbed to spice up our love life.
It doesn't work though!
We've drifted further apart.

What does 'WIFE' stand for?
Washing, Ironing, Food, Etc…

I married my wife for her looks,
but not the one's she's been giving me lately.

What's the difference between prison and marriage?
In prison you get to finish a sentence.

Got my heavy goods licence today.
Or as my wife likes to call it 'marriage certificate.'

The Mrs just went mental at me for not opening the car door for her!
I just panicked and swam to the surface.
Last time I let her drive!

SPOUSE SH!T

My sex doll and I have been together for exactly a year today.
To celebrate our anniversary, I decided to get her a book.
Sex tips for Dummies.

Why should you never take laxatives with Viagra?
It makes you crap in bed!

The Mrs got in the shower with me this morning.
She said "Mmmmm baby, I want you to do bad things to me."
So I put shampoo in her eyes.

Never have a tactical wank before sex!
Trust me; I learnt that the soft way.

Opinions are like orgasms...
Mine is more important, and I don't really care if you have one.

Went to a swinger's party last night in my army uniform.
Had to leave my khakis in the bowl.

What's long and hard and makes women groan?
An ironing board.

Maybe we should tone it down a notch...
The neighbours changed the name of their Wi-Fi network to;
'We can hear you having sex.'

Got a new aftershave called Breadcrumbs.
The birds love it!

SEX SHiT

When I get naked in the bathroom,
the shower usually gets turned on.

You put two fingers in...
Maybe three if it's big enough...
Oh yeah.... now that's how you wash a mug.

If women are so perfect at multi-tasking,
how come they can't have a headache and sex at the same time?

My uncle was jailed for his beliefs.
He believed he could wank on the bus.

The wife asked me what's best thing about a blow job?
I replied, the five minutes of silence.

I've just discovered that my sperm is electrically charged.
It came as a bit of a shock.

Just been in hospital having a large mole removed from my penis.
Won't be trying to shag one of those again.

Last night I reached for my liquid Viagra and accidently
swigged from a bottle of Tippex.
I woke up this morning with a huge correction.

I was snooping through my mum's things and I found a whip,
a mask, and handcuffs. I can't believe it!
My mum's a superhero.

SEX SH!T

They say makeup sex is the best!
I must be doing it wrong though, and now
I've only gone and got a lipstick stuck up my bum.

What's worse than a cardboard box?
Paper tits.

I wanted to have sex with my girlfriend, but she was on her period.
We did it in the end.
I managed to pull some strings.

Having sex in elevators is wrong on so many levels.

A bloke was shagging his overweight Mrs, when his phone rings.
"You'll have to ring me back mate, I'm in the tub" he said.

Don't have phone sex!
You might get hearing aids.

What's the best way to get into a sleeping bag?
Wake her up and give her a kiss.

Two nuns sat on a park bench,
a streaker runs past and flashes them.
One of the nuns has a stroke.
The other couldn't reach.

I'm always Frank with my sexual partners.
Don't want them knowing my real name, do I?!

Our Brazilian housekeeper is rubbish at making the beds.
She's very tidy downstairs though.

Yesterday, a feminist asked me how I view lesbian relationships.
Apparently 'In HD' wasn't the correct answer.

My girlfriend used to smoke after sex.
So we started using lubricant.

If love is blind, why is lingerie so popular?

How do you get a fat woman into bed?
Piece of cake!

What's the difference between a blow job and anal sex?
A blow job makes your day; anal sex makes your hole weak.

What gets longer when pulled,
fits between breasts, inserts neatly in a hole,
and works best when jerked?
A seatbelt.

Two prostitutes discussing the hazards of their job.
"Have you ever been picked up by the fuzz?"
"No, but I've been slung around by the tits."

Two Thai birds asked me to join them for a threesome.
It was just like winning the Lottery!
We had six matching balls.

My girlfriend sent me a 'Get Better Soon' card.
I'm not ill, I'm just not very good at sex.

I was watching porn last night when my mum walked in.
Not the best way to find out what she does for a living.

Life is like a penis.
Simple, relaxed and hanging free.
It's women who make it hard.

Viagra eye drops.
They make you look hard.

If a dove is the bird of peace, what's the bird of love?
Swallow.

A recent survey was conducted into why men like blow jobs:
10% liked the feeling.
12% liked the dominance.
78% liked 5 minutes silence!

My blonde nineteen year old next door neighbour has just asked me
if I know about missing items from her washing line?
I nearly shit her knickers.

SEX SHiT

Ever had sex whilst camping?
It's fucking intents.

Today at the London sperm bank it was a pretty unsuccessful day.
Only two men made appointments.
One came on the bus and the other missed the tube!

What's dangerous and eats nuts?
Syphilis.

Went to a chemist yesterday and said to the pharmacist,
"Excuse me, I'm after some condoms"
"Just a minute" he replied "Yes, that's them."

I don't know why people have sex with women whilst
they are on their period.
It's bloody nuts if you ask me.

I recently suggested to my wife that she should try
masturbating with fruit.
She went fucking bananas.

I got thrown out of a strip club last night for using Monopoly money.
I don't see why I should pay real money to see fake boobs.

I was going to commit suicide by jumping off a cliff;
I looked down and noticed I was above a nudist beach.
So I tossed myself off.

What not to say in a sexy lingerie shop...
"Does this come in kids sizes?"
"No thanks, just sniffing."
"Mum will love this."

SEX SH!T

Welcome to the Sexual Innuendo Club.
Thank you all for coming.

I've been taking Viagra for my sunburn.
It doesn't cure it, but it keeps the sheets off my legs at night.

Give a man a jacket and he'll be warm for a day.
Teach a man to jacket and he'll never leave the house.

I've discovered I have a logic fetish.
I can't stop coming to conclusions.

I splashed out on some new lingerie in the local sex shop.
Now the assistant says I have to pay for it.

What does a Geordie lass use for protection during sex?
A bus shelter!

A furniture store keeps calling me.
All I wanted was one night stand.

I said to my wife, "If you lick my balls I'll come."
She said, "Fuck off, you're going shopping with
me whether you like it or not."

A customer was buying condoms at work today.
I asked if he'd like a bag?
He said, "No, she's not that ugly!"

Had a fight with an erection this morning.
I beat it single handedly!

What's the difference between an egg and a wank?
You can't beat a wank!

What's the difference between a fridge and a fanny?
A fridge doesn't fart when you pull your meat out.

What's the difference between a chickpea and a potato?
You wouldn't pay to have a potato on you.

What's the difference between light and hard?
You can fall asleep with a light on!

I almost had a threesome last night.
I just needed two more people.

I've put a hole in a bar of soap and now I use it to masturbate with.
Normally I wouldn't share this kind of information,
but I just had to... cum clean.

I was on a train and this hot Thai chick sits next to me.
I kept thinking to myself. Please don't get a boner, please!
But she did!

I'm in trouble with my wife after she asked where I was taking her today?
It seems that over the coffee table was not what she wanted to hear.

What did the egg say to the boiling water?
"Sorry, it's going to take me a while to get hard, I got laid last night."

What's green and smells like pork?
Kermit's fingers.

My German girlfriend likes to rate our sex between 1-10.
Last night we tried anal, she kept shouting 9!
That's the best I've done so far.

I'm not really a fan of jokes that use smutty innuendos.
But I do try to slip one in occasionally.

What's the most sensitive part of a man whilst
he's having a sneaky wank?
His ears.

I've been getting anonymous texts from someone telling me
to shower, comb my hair and brush my teeth,
I think they might be trying to groom me.

"Give it to me!" she said
"I'm so fucking wet, give it to me now!"
"Fuck off" I said
"Get your own umbrella."

Why did the Irishman wear two condoms?
To be sure, to be sure!

My mum walked in my room and said, "You'll go blind if you do that!"
I was so embarrassed, I dropped my binoculars
and missed the eclipse.

The words election and erection are spelt similarly.
They both have the same meaning too:
a dick rising to power.

Why do women prefer a man with a circumcised penis?
Because they can't resist anything that has 10% off!

My wife told me: Sex is better on holiday.
Really wasn't a nice postcard to receive.

The postman with a fetish for having sex with mail bags
has now been removed from his post.

I got an email today from a 32 year old bored housewife,
looking for some action.
I've sent her my ironing, that'll keep her busy!

"Dad, why is my sister called Paris?"
"Because we conceived her in Paris."
"Ahh, thanks Dad!"
"You're welcome, Backseat."

I was awakened with a blow job today.
I need to start sleeping with my mouth closed.

What's pink and hard in the morning?
The Financial Times crossword.

When a girl seductively tells you, "You can stick it wherever you want."
Apparently in her sister is NOT one of the options.

How many immature people does it take to screw a light bulb?
Haha, screw!

People ask if I still enjoy sex at 45?
I live at number 57, so it's not far to go.

My penis was in the Guinness Book of Records!
Until the librarian told me to take it out.

Why do men pay more for their car insurance?
Because women don't get blow jobs whilst they're driving.

I was beaten by a woman in a lift.
I was staring at her boobs when she said,
"Would you please press one?"
I don't remember much now.

SEX SHiT

It seems like no matter how much mascara I put on my penis,
I can't seem to make it thicker, fuller or longer lasting.

What's even worse than getting raped by Jack The Ripper?
Being fingered by Captain Hook.

My girlfriend and I just had sex in an apple orchard.
I came in cider.

My girlfriend has a tattoo of a shell on her inner thigh.
If I put my ear to it I can smell the sea.

I'm having a charity event for people that struggle to orgasm.
Let me know if you can't come.

What's the difference between pink and purple?
The grip.

I asked a Chinese girl for her number. She said, "Sex! Sex! Sex!
Free sex tonight!" I said, "Wow!" Then her friend said,
"She means 666-3629."

I had a threesome with a scalene and an isosceles.
It was a love triangle.

I went to the library and asked if they had a book about tiny willies?
Librarian said "I don't think it's in yet?"
I said "Yes, that's the one."

I've decided to marry a pencil.
I can't wait to introduce my parents to my bride 2B.

If it's got tits or wheels, sooner or later you're going to
have problems with it.

Women might be able to fake orgasms,
but men can fake a whole relationship.

My girlfriend thinks I'm a stalker.
Well, she's not actually my girlfriend yet.

What did one light bulb say to the other on Valentine's Day?
I love you watts.

About to watch a film with my girlfriend.
Can anyone recommend a girlfriend?

Learning to love yourself is important.
Just don't let your partner catch you doing it!

February 29th.
The only day that a man doesn't want to see a woman
on her knees in front of him.

20 seconds left on the microwave!
Women: Set the table, pour the wine, tweet, check Facebook.
Men: Start a NASA rocket launch countdown.

I've just phoned and reserved a table to take the Mrs out
on Valentine's night. She will be raging,
she hates snooker!

What gifts do squirrels exchange on Valentine's Day?
Forget-me-nuts.

I'm going on a blind date tonight.
I hope our dogs get on.

What's the difference between a joke and a hot girl?
Sometimes I get the joke.

Men have two emotions: Hungry and Horny.
If you see him without an erection, make him a sandwich.

Love is like a fart.
If you have to force it it's probably shit.

Stages of a relationship:
1) Engagement ring.
2 Wedding ring.
3) Suffer ring.

Just got a new car for my girlfriend.
Great swap.

I told my girlfriend she drew her eyebrows on too high.
She looked surprised.

I met my Mrs at an arthritis support meeting.
You know when two people just click!

All my friends keep saying that my new girlfriend is imaginary.
Joke's on them, so are they!

I went out with a girl called Simile,
I don't know what I metaphor.

She criticised my apartment...
So I knocked her flat.

Nine out of ten men prefer large boobs.
The other man prefers nine men.

My deaf girlfriend was talking in her sleep last night.
She nearly took my fucking eye out!

My girlfriend told me I was one in a million.
When I looked through her text messages,
I had to admit she was right.

What's six inches long has a big purple head
on it and sends women crazy?
A twenty pound note.

Isn't it weird how you see so many more
guys dating guys, and girls dating girls.
I'm just sitting here watching the world go bi.

My Thai Girlfriend assured me that a small penis
should never be an issue in a loving relationship.
I still wish she didn't have one.

Apparently one in three people cheat.
I wonder if it's my wife or my girlfriend?

Last night me and my girlfriend watched three DVDs back to back.
Luckily I was the one facing the telly.

For six years now, I thought my girlfriend had Tourette's.
Turns out I'm actually a fucking twat!

Just broke up with my cross-eyed girlfriend.
She was seeing someone else!

Women only call me ugly until they find out
how much money I make.
Then they call me ugly and poor.

When my girlfriend told me she was pregnant, everything changed.
My name, my address, my phone number.

My ex-girlfriend just text me to say she's made a Voodoo doll of me.
I think she's pulling my leg.

The seven qualities to be the perfect girlfriend are Beautiful, Intelligent,
Gentle, Thoughtful, Innocent, Trustworthy and Sensible.
B.I.G.T.I.T.S.

My mate has got a new epileptic Mrs.
She's well fit.

I'm single through choice,
though not my choice.

My girlfriend left me because I don't take anything seriously.
LMFAO.

My inflatable doll has even left me.
Apparently I let her down.

My girlfriend found out I was cheating,
after she found the letters I was hiding.
She got very upset and won't play Scrabble
with me ever again.

My girlfriend dumped me because of my obsession with plants.
I asked "Where's this stemming from petal?"

Girls are always taking your hoodies, but you take one of their dresses and suddenly they're all like "We need to talk."

What's the difference between Iron Man and Iron Woman?
Iron Man is a superhero.
Iron Woman is a command!

My girlfriend just asked me, "When we go to Egypt,
can we go on a camel?"
I said, "Fuck off, it would take ages to get there on a camel!"

My girlfriend bet me I couldn't do a butterfly impression.
I thought to myself, that's got to be worth a little flutter!

When I see lovers names carved into a tree I don't think it's cute,
I just think it's strange how many people take knives on a date.

Dating Tip:
Swallow magnets to become attractive.

An invisible man marries an invisible woman.
The kids were nothing to look at either!

I've asked my girlfriend to polish my medieval
battle uniform whilst I go to the pub.
She always said she wanted a night in, shining armour.

If you've never rewound a cassette tape with your finger,
you have no right to complain about buffering.

I find it easier to sleep in my son's room in this
hot weather because it's cooler.
He's got a racing car bed and a lava lamp.

What's made of leather and sounds like a sneeze?
A shoe.

As I suspected, someone has been adding soil to my garden.
The plot thickens.

What do you call a girl who sets fire to her credit card statements?
Bernadette.

Me: Mum, am I ugly?
Mum: I've told you not to call me Mum in front of people!

I realised my parents favoured my twin brother when they asked
me to blow up balloons for his surprise birthday party.

My Mum tripped and dropped the basket of clothes she'd just ironed.
It may sound far-fetched but it's true.
I watched it all unfold.

My old man was one to never to go down without a fight.
That's why I'd never get in a lift with him.

I felt like a real gentleman when I opened the door
for the Mother-in-Law the other day.
Mind you, I was doing 60mph at the time.

Singing in the shower is all fun and games
until you get shampoo in your mouth.
Then it just becomes a soap opera.

The Mother-in-Law's drowning, I've informed Emergency Services.
I hope they save her or it's a waste of a first class stamp.

I don't want to sound big-headed but,
I wear a size XXL hat.

I'm not saying my credit record is bad, but the bank wouldn't even
lend me a pen to fill in my loan application!

The guy who stole my diary has died.
My thoughts are with his family.

Saw my Mother-in-Law getting beaten up by five youths earlier!
"Aren't you going to help?" said the wife.
I said "I think five is enough."

Don't waste your money on anti-wrinkle cream.
I have been using it for six months.
My balls still look like walnuts.

I live for my alarm clock collection.
It's the only reason I get up in the morning.

A man tried to sell me a coffin today.
I told him that's the last thing I need.

At weddings old people always poke me and say you'll be next!
It's so annoying!
I've started doing the same to them at funerals.

Do you know what my late father said to me?
Sorry I'm late.

Just found out I have a Chinese half-brother after all these years.
Can't wait to meet Mi Sib Ling.

My mother used to beat me as a child with a camera.
I keep having flashbacks.

We call our Grandad 'Spiderman.'
He hasn't got any superpowers -
he just finds it difficult to get out of the bath.

My recent Google searches:
How to detangle my daughter's hair.
How to detangle a really, really bad tangle.
How to cut out a tangle.
Hats.

My Mother-in-Law's star sign was Cancer,
so it was really ironic how she died.
She was attacked by a giant fucking crab!

My extra sensitive toothpaste doesn't like it
when I use other toothpastes.

My Grandad gave me some sound advice on his deathbed.
He said "It's worth spending money on good speakers."

I guess you all heard about me weeing in the newsagent's yesterday?
It was all over the papers.

Just seen a man slumped over a lawn mower crying his eyes out.
He said he'll be fine, he's just going through a rough patch.

I bought a vacuum cleaner six months ago and so far
all it's been doing is gathering dust.

I went by the house I grew up in and asked if I could go
in and look around. They said no and slammed the door!
My parents can be so rude.

The Mother-in-Law has been admitted into hospital for shoving
a vacuum hoover attachment up her fanny.
Doctors say she's picking up nicely!

My cousin Tommy drowned the other day.
At his funeral, we placed a life-jacket on his coffin.
It's what he would have wanted.

I want to die peacefully in my sleep, like my Grandfather.
Not screaming and yelling like the passengers in his car.

My uncle just lost both hands in a horrible accident.
I can't even begin to imagine how he feels.

I offered my Nan £5 for a go on her stair lift.
I thinks she's going to take me up on it.

"We never had a TV in the family when
I was younger" said my Grandad.
"Well you have now" I said as I adjusted my dress.

I took the Mother-in-Law out the other night.
I love being a sniper.

As a child, my Mum told me I could be anyone I wanted to be.
Turns out, this is called 'Identity Theft.'

I asked my Grandad if he could still do a handstand?
He only lasted about two seconds before
unintentionally tea-bagging himself.

I can't believe Pretzels are knot-bread.

My girlfriend disliked my obsession with Japanese food.
Sushi left me.

I used to date a girl who worked in a brewery and only had one leg.
She was in charge of the hops!

If you see someone doing a crossword today, lean over
them and say 7 up is Lemonade.

We live in a society where pizza gets to your house before the police.

For lunch tomorrow, I'm having a bun filled with ham and pineapple.
That's Hawaii roll.

RIP boiled water.
You will be mist.

I swallowed some food colouring. My doctor says I'm ok,
but I feel like I've dyed a little on the inside.

FOR SALE:
Packet of Polo's.
Unopened.
Mint condition.

I was eating my tea last night when I suddenly thought to myself...
this milk must be seriously out of date.

Mushrooms.
The breakfast of champignons.

Burnt my Hawaiian pizza today.
Should have put it on aloha setting!

We've been trying to think of some vegetable jokes.
If you can think of any, lettuce know.

My girlfriend laughed at me when I said I had a car made from spaghetti.
You should've seen her face when I drove pasta.

What do you call an Alien who eats too much cheese,
egg yolks and animal fat?
An extra-cholesterol.

Have you heard about the evil group of men who control
all the world's cheese?
The Hallouminati!

I just opened a kitchen cupboard and loads of
Omega 3 capsules fell on my head.
I'm alright though, just some superfishoil injuries.

I just bought some of that coconut shampoo.
I don't know why, I've not got a coconut.

There's been an explosion at a pie factory in Melton Mowbray.
3.14159265 dead.

I love cooking children and dogs.
But I hate using commas.

I can give you one vegetable joke about onions.
But that's shallot.

Went to the butchers to play poker last week.
Left after an hour, the steaks were too high.

I called my dad from the shop saying I'd forgotten what
orange juice he asked for. "Concentrate" he said,
but I still couldn't remember!

Whilst cooking today I accidentally rubbed some herbs in my eyes.
I'm now parsley sighted.

I've just spilt my onion milk.
I've never cried so much in my life.

I used to be addicted to eating soap.
But I'm clean now.

What type of music does cheese like best?
R & Brie.

My winter fat has gone.
I now have spring rolls.

Knowledge is knowing a tomato is a fruit.
Wisdom is not putting it in a fruit salad.

Two peanuts walking down the road.
One was a salted.

I bought some pork chops and told the butcher to make them lean.
He said, 'Which way?'

Some guy just assaulted me with milk, cream and butter.
How dairy!

My friends were amazed when I told them I can predict the future
using herbs. "Is it true?" they asked.
"Only thyme will tell", I replied.

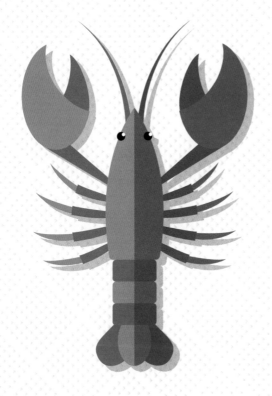

I ate at Mary Poppin's restaurant today.
Super cauliflower cheese but the lobster was atrocious.

Having a massage....
Lady said "Any extras?"
I said "No, get your own chewing gum."

What do you call a fake noodle?
An Impasta.

I went out and had ten pints of yoghurt last night.
I was well Muller'd.

What's the worst vegetable to bring on a boat?
A leek.

Bloke: Waiter what is this fly doing in my soup?
Waiter: I do believe that's backstroke sir.

What's long and thin, covered in skin, red in parts, and goes in tarts?
Rhubarb.

Many people are worrying about the effects
of genetically modified crops.
"There is no proof of any adverse effects" said one carrot.

This girl came up to me today and said she
recognised me from Vegetarian Club.
I was confused, I'd never met herbivore.

I'm about to have a cup of dangerous coffee.
Safe tea first though.

Did you hear about the French cheese factory that exploded?
There was de Brie everywhere.

What did the cheese say when it looked in the mirror?
"Halloumi."

What cheese is made backwards?
Edam.

What cheese would you use to hide a small horse?
Mascarpone.

What cheese do you use to lure a bear down a mountain?
Camembert.

How do you approach an angry Welsh cheese?
Caerphilly.

Tried to sign up to a website the other day.
I put my password as "beef stew"
but it said password wasn't stroganoff.

FOOD AND DRINK SHiT

I just ate a frozen apple.
Hardcore.

I used to know how to make those little fizzy sweets but then I forgot.
So I went on a Refresher course!

I wrote a song about a tortilla.
Well actually, it's more of a wrap.

What's Batman's favourite fruit?
BA-NA-NA-NA-NA-NA-NA-NA BA-NA-NA-NA-NA-NA-NA-NA
Grapefruit.

I always found the fishmonger at my local market
to be a little standoffish.

What's the fastest cake in the world?
Scone.

Just managed to burn 2000 calories in 30 minutes!
The pizza's ruined though.

Chinese takeaway - £9
Delivery charge - £1
Realising the idiots have forgot one of your containers - Riceless.

Why did the mushroom go to the party?
It didn't. Do you know why?
Because it's a fucking mushroom.

What do you call cheese that is not yours?
Nacho cheese.

What begins with T, ends with T, and has T in it?
A teapot.

Just got a birthday card, opened it and a Yorkshire pudding fell out!
It was from my Aunt Bessie.

Just been to Tesco and swapped fifty raisins for one hundred sultanas.
Can't believe the currant exchange rate!

Just got a birthday card, opened it and rice went everywhere!
It was from my Uncle Ben!

A Roman walks into a bar, holds up two fingers,
and says, "Five beers please."

How does Moses make his tea?
Hebrews it.
I'm serious that Israeli how he does it.

I'm making a fruit salad and the recipe says
'Pineapples - Five cubed.'
Where on earth am I going to get 125 pineapples?

Just had some people at my door trying to convince me that
brown bread was better than white bread.
They were Hovis witnesses.

I went to a cannibal restaurant last night.
£50 a head.

I threw a biscuit at my neighbour the other day, but he ducked.
Jammy Dodger.

Life is like a box of chocolates.
It doesn't last long if you're fat bastard.

When I found out that my toaster wasn't waterproof,
I was shocked!

I just ate my alarm clock,
it was so time consuming.

Last night I watched a documentary on a guy who worked
sixty hours a week crushing coke cans.
It was soda pressing.

I went into a cake shop today and asked,
"Is that a custard or a meringue?"
She said "You're not wrong, it's a custard."

Did you hear about the terrible accident at Spaghetti Junction?
Twelve people were injured, and three pastaway.

Stop being mean to fat people!
They have enough on their plate.

Where does a vegetarian go on holiday?
Quornwall.

Tea is for mugs.

My five year old old son was expelled from school for race crime.
He used glue on his egg and spoon.

I went to the pub earlier and had a ploughmans lunch.
He went fucking mental.

Bought my mum a fridge for her birthday.
You should've seen her face light up when she opened it!

My girlfriend wanted perfume and jewellery for her birthday,
but I got her a chocolate egg and a toy instead.
She was kinder surprised.

People laugh at my car because it's ugly and green.
But at least I avocado.

FOOD AND DRINK SHiT

I went to a seafood disco last night.
I pulled a mussel.

I drove past my gran's house this morning and saw
eleven pints of milk on her doorstep. I thought,
"She must be thirsty today."

Went to the shop the other day to buy six cans of Sprite.
Only when I got home did I realise I'd picked 7up.

Why did the banana go to the doctors?
Because he wasn't peeling very well.

Saw the world's largest egg earlier.
I thought that will take some beating.

Did you hear about the guy who got hit
in the head with a can of cola?
He was lucky it was a soft drink.

What happens to an egg when you tell it a joke?
It cracks up!

I discovered that I have an amazing talent today.
I found I can melt ice cubes just by staring at them,
it takes a few hours though.

How do eggs leave the motorway?
By using the eggs it!

What day do eggs hate the most?
Fry days!

What do you call a chicken in a shell suit?
An egg.

I was told that you could view a solar eclipse through a colander?
I tried it and ended up straining my eyes.

They say the way to a man's heart is through his stomach.
Unless he's a vegan.
Then you can get there through his vagina.

When is a door not a door?
When it's ajar.

What do you get if you pour boiling water down a rabbit hole?
A hot cross bunny.

"How's the diet going?" I asked my mate
"Not good" he sighed, "I had ten eggs for breakfast this morning"
"Oh dear", "Fried?"
"No, Chocolate"

After exercise I always eat a pizza!
Just kidding, I don't exercise.

My friend thinks he is smart.
He told me an onion is the only food that can make you cry,
so I threw a coconut at his face.

What do you call a bear with no teeth?
A gummy bear.

What kind of tea is hard to swallow?
Reality.

A guy just knocked on my door and asked
who my energy supplier was.
Apparently Red Bull wasn't the answer he was looking for.

The man that invented throat lozenges died last week.
There was no coffin at the funeral.

For my next trick, I will eat a musical instrument in a bread bap.
Drum roll please.

Just been thrown out of cinema for taking my own food,
been ages since I've had a barbecue.

I asked my butcher to pass me down two cuts
of sirloin from the top shelf.
He refused as the "Steaks were too high."

Bucket list:
1) Bucket.
2) Ice.
3) Beer.

Why did the Mexican push his wife off the cliff?
Tequila.

Female wanted; must have own pub.
Apply with inn.

I doubt Vodka is the answer, but it's worth a shot!

This bloke just came in my workplace shouting "Vodka, tequila, sambuca!
I said "Hey! I call the shots round here!"

I got chatting to a lumberjack in a pub.
He seemed like a decent feller.

What's the best thing for a hangover?
Drink loads the night before.

Dad's advice some years ago;
"If you get into a fight in the pub, put a snooker ball in your sock."
Worst advice ever, I could hardly walk!

Fucking hell its windy out there.
Only went out to get the Mrs some bread and got blown into the pub.

What's the difference between a dog and a fox?
About nine pints.

My Grandad was an alcoholic.
We called him alchopops.

My mate lost an arm to a snake bite.
He had twelve pints of it and fell through a window.

Beauty is in the eye of the beer-holder.

I just drank some WKD with ice in it.
It was wicked.

Today I have officially been sober for one hundred days.
Not like, in a row or anything, just in total.

I fell asleep at a party last night, and someone put
a teabag in my mouth, I went mental!
No one treats me like a mug.

My grandad is 93 and still doesn't need glasses!
He just drinks straight from the bottle.

What do you call a drunk dinosaur?
A staggersaurus.

As I looked into her eyes I felt my knees go weak
and my stomach turned to butterflies.
That's when I realised I'd drugged the wrong glass.

Quasimodo goes to the pub and says "Scotch whiskey please"
Barman says "Bell's alright?"
Quasi says "Mind your own business."

Got arrested last night for refusing to pay my bar tab.
Apparently at Club Tropicana the drinks aren't free.

You're all invited to my recycling party on Saturday at 8pm.
Bring a bottle or a few cans.

There's a new craze in the UK where men are drinking vodka
from a woman's fanny with a straw!
The government fears a rise in minge drinking.

It's not my fault I have a double-chin...
When God was giving out chins, I thought he said Gin,
so I said I'll have a double.

Because of the hot weather my boss has said we can bring shorts in, whiskey it is then!

I found my wife slumped over Hadrian's Wall with an empty vodka bottle in her hand.
I think she might be a borderline alcoholic!

Alcoholic man seeks similar woman to have a drink or two, maybe more.

Alcohol is never the answer; it just makes you forget the question.

I got so drunk last night I started a fight with a mop.
To be fair I wiped the floor with him.

My mates reckon that I'll find any excuse to have a drink.
Speaking of beer…

Alcohol probably won't fix your problems.
But it's worth a shot.

Saw a guy zig zagging in the streets late last night shouting
"Vodka, Vodka, Vodka!"
I thought that's the spirit.

Despite getting A-level results of A, B, B, A it seems that no employer will take a chance on me.

If you're a hostage and the gunman says "Who shall I shoot first?" Saying, "It's WHOM shall I shoot first?" Is not the best answer.

I really like the name Saturn.
It has a lovely ring to it.

My poor knowledge of Greek mythology has always been my Achilles elbow.

People tell me that my grammar stinks...
What do they expect? She's 89.

---

19 and 20 had a fight. 21.

I remember at school when we discussed the great rulers.
I opted for the Helix 30cm shatterproof.

Feeling cold today?
Go and stand in a corner for a bit.
They are usually around 90 degrees.

I'm having my first violin lesson today.
It's a bit fiddly.

There's a thin line between a numerator and denominator.
Only a fraction of people will find this funny.

I heard that Oxygen and Magnesium are going out.
I was like OMg.

3.14% of sailors are Pi Rates.

School phoned and said my son's been lying.
I said, "Tell him he's very good, I haven't got any kids."

I put a wooden desk and a blackboard in my living room.
To make it look more classy.

I've taken up speed reading. I can read 'War and Peace' in 20 seconds.
It's only 3 words but it's a start.

Know any jokes about Sodium?
Na.

First rule of Thesaurus Club.
You don't talk, converse, discuss, speak, chat, deliberate,
confer, gab, gossip or natter about Thesaurus Club.

Me and my mate were fighting over which was the best vowel.
I won!

It wasn't school that I hated,
just the Principal of it.

I've failed maths so many times I've lost count!

If pronouncing my b's as v's makes me sound Russian, then Soviet.

The rotation of earth really makes my day.

At university I was going to join the debating team,
but someone talked me out of it!

The past and the present walked into a bar.
It was tense.

A man walks into a library and asks for a book on Tourette's.
Librarian: "Fuck off, you twat!"
Man: "Yes that's the one!"

Astronomers got tired of watching the
moon go round the earth for 24 hours.
So they decided to call it a day.

What did the scientist say when he found two helium atoms?
HeHe.

How often do I make chemistry jokes?
Periodically.

I'd make a good chemistry pun, but all the good ones Argon.

What's the best thing about Switzerland?
I don't know, but their flag is a huge plus.

A hypnotist convinced me I was a soft, malleable metal
with an atomic number of eighty-two.
I'm easily lead.

A man goes into a library and asks for a book on suicide.
The librarian replies "Fuck off, you won't bring it back."

Dear student loan, thank you for saving my life.
I can't think how I will ever repay you.

Some helium floats into a bar and tries to order a drink.
The barman says, "We don't serve noble gases in here."
The helium doesn't react.

Scientists have discovered that people will believe anything as
long as you start a sentence by saying,
'Scientists have discovered that.'

Thanks for explaining the word "many" to me,
it means a lot.

The amount of people who confuse 'to' and 'too' is amazing two me.

Why is abbreviation such a long word?

Whiteboards are remarkable.

I'll stop at nothing to avoid using negative numbers.

Did you hear about the cross eyed teacher?
She couldn't control her pupils!

Sometimes I use big words which I don't understand
to make me seem more photosynthesis.

Don't trust atoms.
They make up everything.

Last time I was someone's type, I was donating blood.

When you get a bladder infection, urine trouble.

What's the difference between an oral and a rectal thermometer?
The taste.

I can get you five thousand tampax for a fiver.
No strings attached.

Spent all of my wages on skin cream.
Bit of a rash decision!

Guess who I bumped into in the opticians today?
Everybody.

I hate being bipolar,
it's amazing.

I've just been diagnosed with Hypochondria.
I knew something was wrong with me.

My Auntie Marge has been in hospital for weeks.
I can't believe she's not better.

Just phoned the hospital asking about how my best mate was doing?
He swallowed a £2 coin last night.
Still no change.

The doctor recently diagnosed me with '70s Fever'
It flares up occasionally.

Doctors tell us that there's 10,000,000 overweight people in the UK.
These are of course just round figures.

"Doctor, Doctor, I think I need glasses."
"You certainly do, this is a fish and chip shop."

I wasn't originally going to get a brain transplant,
but then I changed my mind.

I saw a woman wearing a t-shirt with "Guess" on it.
I said "Implants?"

"What do we want?"
"A CURE FOR PARANOIA"
"When do we want it?"
"WHO WANTS TO KNOW?"

I'm going to appear on Embarrassing Bodies later.
One of my testicles is considerably bigger than the other two!

I went to the doctors because everywhere I pressed hurt.
Pressed my leg it hurt, pressed my arm it hurt, my head it hurt.
Turns out I'd broken my finger.

Dentists are going on strike.
Brace yourselves.

Did you know diarrhea is hereditary?
It runs in your jeans!

Did you hear about the man with five willies?
His underpants fit like a glove!

Me: Doctor you've got to help me, I'm addicted to Twitter.
Doctor: I don't follow you.

I asked the librarian if they had any books on paranoia?
She whispered, "They're behind you."

I wish I had a pair of skinny genes.

"Doctor, I think I'm a moth."
"It's not a doctor you need, it's a psychiatrist."
"I was on my way there when I saw your light on!"

Son: Mum, don't get scared but I'm calling you from the hospital
Mum: Son, you've been a doctor for four years
and you still go on with that shit!

Dogs can't operate MRI machines,
but catscan.

They say time is a great healer.
That's probably why when you go to the doctors surgery
they keep you waiting so long.

My biology teacher grew human vocal chords from stem cells in the lab.
The results speak for themselves.

I said to the doctor, "Can you give me something for my liver?"
He gave me a pound of onions.

My doctor said to me, "Do you know your sperm count?"
I said, "I didn't know they were that clever!"

A man woke up in hospital after an accident.
He shouted "Doctor, I can't feel my legs!"
The Doctor replied "I know you can't, I've cut off your arms!"

Comas can really change the meaning of a sentence...
For instance:
"Ben is in a hurry."
"Ben is in a coma."

My doctor just told me I was suffering from paranoia.
He didn't actually say that, but I could tell it was
what the bastard was thinking.

You know what makes me smile?
Facial muscles.

I said to the doctor:
"The older I get, the more I spread gossip."
He said: "That's Rumourtism."

Just been to my local hospital and I saw a sign saying
'Thieves Operate Here.'
Surely it would be safer to leave it to the Surgeons?

Yawning is your bodies way of saying 20% battery remaining.

If Dave has fifty chocolate bars and eats forty five,
what does he have left?
Diabetes.

A man walks into a psychiatrist's office wearing shorts
made of Clingfilm. The shrink says
"Well, I can see your nuts!"

I went to the doctors the other day and I said,
"Have you got anything for wind?"
He gave me a kite.

Boy asks Grandad; "Have you seen my pills,
they were labelled LSD?"
Grandad replies; "Fuck the pills, have you seen
the dragons in the kitchen?"

A friend of mine just told me that she's got swelling
on her arse, legs and boobs...
I thought that's far too much inflammation!

I went to the doctors with hearing problems.
He said "Can you describe the symptoms?"
I said "Homers a fat bloke and Marge has blue hair"

Did you hear about the blind circumciser?
He got the sack!

The boss of a paint company has died of hypothermia
whilst trekking across the Antarctic.
Medics say he needed a second coat.

Why did the Doctor tiptoe past the medicine cabinet?
Because he didn't want to wake the sleeping pills!

I've developed a taste for fabric conditioner.
My doctor says I'm fine, I've just been comfort eating.

A woman weightlifter goes to the doc's:
"I've been taking steroids, and now I've grown a cock"
"Anabolic" says the Doctor
"No just a cock."

Doctor: "I'm sorry but you have a terminal illness and have only ten to live" Patient: "What do you mean, ten? Ten what? Months? Weeks?!"
Doctor: "Nine."

I took the batteries out of my carbon monoxide detector today.
The loud beeping was giving me a headache and
making me feel sick and dizzy.

My sister asked me if I wanted to wind her new born baby?
I thought that's a bit harsh, so I just gave him a dead leg instead.

What's long, hard, bendable and contains the letters p, e, n, i, s?
Your spine.

This is what I like about chiropractors...
They always have your back.

What do you call a man with no shins?
Tony.

My doctor wrote me a prescription for dailysex.
But my girlfriend insists it says dyslexia.

"I stand corrected", said the man in orthopaedic shoes.

Bursts into doctor's surgery!
Me: "I'm no longer canstopetid"
Doc: "You mean constipated?"
Me: "No, I've had a vowel movement"
Doc: "Get out!"

My girlfirend got confused and went to see
a tree surgeon instead of a plastic surgeon.
Mind you, she does have a very nice bush now.

A bloke just offered me forty grand a year
to work for him at the brittle bones society.
I snapped his hand off.

My mate swallowed his phone and got it stuck in his throat.
I had to ring his neck.

How often do I make menstruation jokes?
Periodically.

"Doctor Doctor, I feel like a window."
"Can you tell me where the pane is?"

I'm seeing this girl with eczema.
She's got a cracking body.

How can you tell which nurse is the head nurse?
It's the one with dirty knees.

Paddy on a First Aid Course;
Instructor asks "What would you do if your child
swallowed the front door key?"
Paddy "Climb through the window!"

Psychic wanted: You know where to apply.

Went for a job as a potato packer.
Ended up getting the sack.

Started a band called 999 Megabytes
We haven't got a gig yet.

Just got a new job as a waiter.
The pay isn't great, but it puts food on the table.

My dad used to say "Always fight fire with fire."
Which is probably why he got thrown out of the fire brigade.

I used to be a tap dancer but I kept falling in the sink.

I hate perforated lines,
they're tearable.

Whoever stole my copy of Office,
I will hunt you down and I will make you pay!
You have my Word!

I recently lost my job as a teacher.
I got caught shagging the ugliest teacher in the whole school.
Gross Miss Conduct.

My dad's bread factory burnt down.
Now his business is toast.

My boss hates it when I shorten his name to Dick!
Especially as his name is Matthew.

Why was the broom late for work?
Because he overswept.

No matter how much you push the envelope,
it'll still be stationary.

A spider just crawled onto my keyboard.
Don't worry, it's under ctrl.

I've started a business building yachts in my attic.
Sails are going through the roof!

If a tree falls in the forest and nobody hears it...
Then my illegal logging business is a success!

Boss: Stop copy and pasting your responses from old emails.
Me: No problem.
Sent from my iPhone
Sent from my iPhone

I was going to nail a shelf to my wall...
but then I thought, screw it!

The 21st century:
Where deleting history is more important than making it.

Why did the feminist refuse to work at the post office?
Because it was a mail dominated industry.

The Internet has become too politically correct,
What's all this nonsense about disabled cookies?
In my day they were called broken biscuits.

Tried changing my password to "14days"
but it was two week.

I walked down a street where the houses were numbered
64K, 128K, 256K, 512K and 1MB.
That was a trip down memory lane.

The guy who invented predictive text passed away yesterday.
His funfair will be next monkey.

I remember the days when Blue Ray was an elderly gentleman
who drowned in our local swimming pool.

Why did the baker rob the bank?
Because he kneaded the dough.

I used to work in a shoe recycling shop.
It was sole destroying.

I love pressing F5.
It's so refreshing.

I used to be a banker but I lost interest.

I had a really funny joke, but autocorrect ruined the lunchtime.

Therapist: "What would you say to your dad if he were alive today?"
"Sorry for cremating you, I honestly thought you were dead."

I failed my audition as Romeo through
a misunderstanding over a stage direction.
My copy of the script said: "Enter Juliet from the rear."

Rang work earlier and said "I won't be in tomorrow, I'm sick."
The boss said "How sick are you?"
I said "I'm in bed with my Grandma."

Just purchased some shoes from a drug dealer.
I don't know what he laced them with
but I've been tripping all day.

One-armed butlers.
They can take it but they can't dish it out.

I've started my new job as a settee salesman today...
Sofa so good.

Want to hear a construction joke?
I'm working on it.

If you want a job in the moisturiser industry,
the best advice I can give is to apply daily.

What do you call a fat psychic?
A four-chin teller.

Archaeology really is a career in ruins.

My window cleaner was banging on my window shouting and swearing!
I thought to myself: He's lost his rag.

Knock knock. Who's there?
The postman.
The postman who?
Look, do you want this parcel or not?

A salesman knocked on my door yesterday and said,
"Who currently provides your internet?"
I said, "My next door neighbour."

Why did the baker have brown hands?
Because he kneaded a poo.

I've just been shouted at for having a mass debate in the office.
From tomorrow, no more mass debating in work!

Nobody expected our window cleaner to kick the bucket.

Went to the job centre yesterday and asked
if they had any furniture removal jobs?
They told me to "Take a seat."

Payslips are like willies. Although you don't go around comparing
yours to other peoples, you always hope it's a little bigger.

I can hear music coming out of my printer.
I think the paper's jammin' again.

A bus station is where a bus stops.
A train station is where a train stops.
On my desk, I have a work station.

I started my new job this morning shifting leaves.
I'm raking it in!

A bloke on a tractor has just driven past me shouting
"The end of the world is nigh!"
I think it was Farmer Geddon.

I got sacked from my job as a theatre designer.
I left without making a scene.

My boss just announced he's going to fire
the employee with the worst posture.
I've a hunch it could be me.

Who can shave twenty five times a day and still have a beard?
A barber!

I didn't want to think my dad stole from his construction job
but when I got home all the signs were there.

I once went for a job as a gold prospector,
but it didn't pan out.

I started a company selling land mines that look like prayer mats.
Prophets are going through the roof.

Yesterday at a job interview I filled my glass of water until it
overflowed a little. Interviewer: "Nervous?"
Me: "No, I always give 110%."

"Does this uniform make me look fat?"
Insecurity Guard.

What do lawyers wear to court?
Law suits.

I just got asked the time by a British Gas repair man.
So I told the bastard it was between 8am and 1pm!

Drilling for oil is boring.

I wish there was some way to identify idiots online.
Sent from my iPhone.

I have a new job, I'm helping a one armed typist with capital letters.
It's shift work.

Just invented a new flavour of crisps.
If they're successful I'll make a packet.

The computers were down at work today,
so we had to do everything manually.
It took me twenty minutes to shuffle the cards to play solitaire.

My mates just got a job at the dentist.
I said, "Is it full time?"
He said, "No, I'm just filling in."

My grandfather was a baker for the army.
When he went to war, he went in all buns glazing.

I used to be a freelance journalist, but I wasn't very good at it.
Lance is still in prison.

I am going to apply for a job as a waiter.
I could bring a lot to the table.

Why did the scarecrow get a promotion?
Because he was outstanding in his field.

What's Forrest Gump's Password?
1Forrest1

I got asked today "Who would you most like to be stuck in a lift with?"
I said "Obviously a lift engineer."

I told my boss that I needed a pay rise, I said that three other
companies were after me. Boss "Which ones?"
I replied "The gas, electric and the water."

I met somebody at work today called William Hill.
What are the odds?

Always follow your dreams.
Except for that one where you're naked at work.

I used to have a mate who had a business in origami.
It's folded now.

I think my spell Czech is broken.

Why did the policeman go to sleep?
Because he needed arrest!

Always trust a glue salesman.
They always stick to their word

Failed a job interview last week.
Apparently a gangbang isn't proof you can work in a team.

I asked my boss, "Where do you want this big roll of bubble wrap?"
He said, "Just pop it over there in the corner."
It took me three hours.

I had to quit my job at the orange juice factory.
I just couldn't concentrate.

Breaking News: A mass fight has broken out in a petrol station.
Twenty three people arrested in Total!

My next-door neighbour worships exhaust pipes,
he's a catholic converter.

I asked my North Korean friend how it was there,
he said he couldn't complain.

I took the rear view mirror out of my car, and since then
I've never looked back.

I got really emotional this morning at the petrol station. I don't know why
I just started filling up.

I met a Dutch girl with inflatable shoes last week,
phoned her up to arrange a date but unfortunately
she'd popped her clogs.

I stopped at the petrol station to pump up my tyres
and noticed that the price was now £1!
Oh well, that's inflation for you I suppose.

My mum always used to say "40 is the new 30"
Lovely woman, banned from driving.

My car failed it's emissions test today!
Fuming.

I was driving on the motorway yesterday in a hearse.
Police pulled me over for undertaking.

Why couldn't the bicycle stand up by itself?
It was two-tyred.

What's a twack?
Something a twain wuns on.

My uncle works for a company that makes bicycle wheels.
He's the Spokesman.

A man took an airline to court after his luggage went missing.
Unfortunately he lost his case!

I've been watching a ship being built.
It was riveting.

I will never forget my childhood summers, when we would climb
inside old tyres and roll down the hills.
They were goodyears.

I used to date a tennis player...
But love meant nothing to her.

To stay in shape my grandma started walking
five miles a day when she was 60.
She's 97 today and we don't know where the hell she is.

A kitchen knife and fork had a race.
Who won? Neither.
It ended in a drawer.

I went to the park with a boomerang yesterday,
but couldn't remember how to throw it.
Then it came back to me.

If you have a referee in football, what do you have in bowls?
Cornflakes.

My mate used liquorice as bait when he went fishing.
He caught all sorts!

I saw a group of neighbours jogging past my house and it really
inspired me to get up and close the blinds.

I went bobsleighing last night.
Killed fifteen people called Bob.

Men at 26 play football, men at 40 play tennis, men at 60 plays golf.
Have you noticed every time you get older
your balls gets smaller?

Who will take the second shot in this epic game of snooker?
We'll find out after the break.

If there's one thing that makes me throw up
it's a dartboard on the ceiling!

What do you call a nervous javelin thrower?
Shakespeare.

Why do scuba divers always fall backwards out of the boat?
Because if they fell forwards, they'd still be in the boat.

Do gun manuals have a trouble-shooting section?

Just got back from the funeral of the man killed by a tennis ball.
It was a cracking service.

I've started a new workout routine this week.
Every day I do diddly-squats.

Saw a golf buggy parked in a disabled bay
this morning and thought to myself;
I wonder what his handicap is?

What time does Andy Murray go to bed?
Tennish.

Exercise bikes get you nowhere.

I'm so strong I can lift buildings!
Well...only if it's a lighthouse.

Does anyone want to join my javelin club?
I'm just throwing it out there.

I love rowing.
It's oarsome.

My girlfriend can't wrestle,
but you should see her box!

I gave up playing rugby at school.
All the teachers kept saying was "Nice try."

I wondered why the football was getting bigger.
Then it hit me.

Shame to hear that Johnstone's Paint are ending their
association with the Football League Trophy.
I'm actually quite emulsional about it.

Did you hear about the angry gymnast?
He just flipped.

Today a man knocked on my door and asked for a small
donation towards the school swimming pool.
I gave him a glass of water.

I've been really busy teaching hobbits how to play cricket.
Bilbo's good at catching, but he can't
really Frodo!

Me and my limbo teammates go way back.

What's the toughest part of the Chinese Marathon?
That moment you hit the wall.

What's the most difficult thing about roller-skating?
Telling your mum and dad you're gay.

Went to the gym and found a new machine.
Used it for an hour and felt sick, its good though, it does everything!
Chocolate, crisps and sweets.

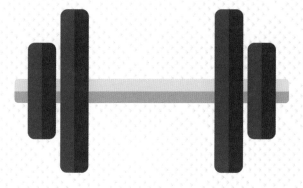

I've just broken up with my gym.
We were just not working out.

A hot girl came up to me in a bar and said,
"Do you want me to show you good time?"
I said, "Yes yes yes!"
Then she ran 100m in 9.23 seconds.

One of the Russian acrobats in our human pyramid has been deported.
We didn't have Oleg to stand on.

I've been trying to teach my mate how to play golf recently
but the problem seems to be his drive.
His wife stands on it and doesn't let us out.

I feel really bad for the Mexican Olympian disqualified
from weightlifting for excessive use of protein.
They told him, "No whey, Jose."

I promised myself I wouldn't masturbate during the Olympics,
but once the women's volleyball came on I was gripped.

Did you hear about the athlete who tested positive for Viagra?
He tripped over during the 100m sprint
and won gold in the pole vault.

Why doesn't Mexico have a good Olympic team?
Because anyone that can run, jump or swim is in the USA.

After giving my son two karate lessons,
he said he didn't want any more.
Still, at least I got my car washed and my fence painted.

Paddy climbs the diving board with a fish.
The official says: "What are you doing with that fish Paddy?"
Paddy: "Triple somersault with pike."

What's the only reason Donald Trump is watching the Olympics?
So he can determine how high Mexican pole vaulters can jump.

I found a hole in my trainer that's big enough to put my finger through.
One complaint from her, and I'm now banned from the gym.

Breaking News! Seven wheelchair athletes
have been banned from the Paralympics
after they tested positive for WD40.

Just been watching the Olympic Ladies Beach Volleyball
and there's already been a wrist injury!
I should be ok for the final.

What happens if you go on a survival course and you don't pass?

I was told that exercise helps with your decision making.
It's true. After going to the gym earlier
I've decided I'm never going again.

Breaking News:
The Irish fencing team have withdrawn from the Olympics already!
They've ran out of creosote!

Went swimming earlier, I had a wee in the deep end.
Lifeguard blew his whistle so loud I nearly fell in!

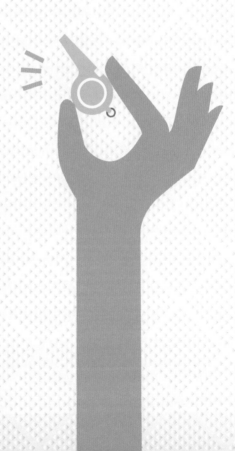

What do you call a woman who stands between two goal posts?
Annette.

I've just been attacked by a little ginger boy doing martial arts!
It turned out to be the carroty kid.

Old yachtsmen don't die... they just keel over.

I can't think of any boat jokes.
Canoe?

I had an argument with my friend about his small boat.
We fell out.

A bad football team is like an old bra,
no cups and very little support.

The position of your hands is very important when playing golf.
I position mine to cover up my scorecard.

If you shot someone with a starting gun,
would you get done for race crimes?

Some people think there are insects on the Moon.
Lunar tics.

I was recently on safari in the Serengeti and witnessed
two male lions shagging. I thought blimey,
have they got no pride?

I told my cat I was going to teach him to speak English.
He looked at me and said "Me how?"

What's the difference between a piano and a fish?
You can tune a piano but you can't tuna fish!

How do frogs die?
They Kermit suicide.

Where do you take a frog with bad eyesight?
To the hoptician.

Whats red and white and sits in a tree?
A sanitary owl.

As I watched the dog chase his tail, I thought
"Dogs are easily amused." Then I realised
I was watching the dog chase his tail.

Why does a milking stool have only 3 legs?
Because the cow has the udder.

What do you do if you come across a tiger in the jungle?
Wipe it off and apologise.

It really bugs me when people use insect puns.

My cat is recovering after a massive stroke.

A friend of mine tried to annoy me with bird puns,
but I soon realised that toucan play at that game.

Stable relationships are for horses.

What do you call a monkey in a mine field?
A baboom.

I know a man who taught his dog to play the
trumpet on the London Underground.
He went from Barking to Tooting in an hour.

What do you call a big pile of cats?
A meowntain.

Ketamine - just say neigh.

Never moon a werewolf

I always thought I had a massive cock.
Turned out to be an ostrich.

What's the last thing that goes through a fly's mind
when it hits the windscreen?
It's arse!

What do you call an aardvark that's just been beaten up?
Vark.

I just watched a programme about beavers.
It was the best dam programme I've ever seen!

I'm very good at remembering random facts.
For example, there are 3,500 different types of lice.
And that's just off the top of my head.

What do you call an elephant that doesn't matter?
An irrelephant.

Two whales walk into a bar.
The first one says, "Weeeeeoooooouuuhhhh".
The next whale says, "Shut up, Steve. You're drunk."

I saw this bloke chatting up a cheetah.
I thought, "he's trying to pull a fast one"

I tried water polo but my horse drowned.

Fisherman walks into a bar with his prize catch.
Barman, "Why the long plaice?"

I've named my dog "ten miles"
Just so I can tell people I walk ten miles twice a day.

Whenever a bird shits on my car, I eat a plate
of scrambled eggs on my front porch,
just to let them know what I'm capable of.

I went to my local bookstore and asked the woman
for a book about turtles.
She asked "Hardback?" and I was like
"Yeah, and little heads."

My wife bought a Siamese Cat.
Weird scary face, big ugly eyes, shits in the garden a lot and scowls,
but she's an adoring wife.

Where did Noah keep the Bees?
In the ark-hives.

Why can't you hear a pterodactyl using the bathroom?
Because the P is silent.

Butterflies just aren't what they used to be.

When I was young I used to think Earwigs actually lived in your ears!
You can imagine how terrified I was of cockroaches!

If carrots are so good for the eyes,
why are there so many dead rabbits on our roads?

What do you get if you insert human DNA into a hamster?
Banned from the pet store.

How do you circumcise a whale?
Send in four skin divers.

A lady carrying a duck walks into a bar.
Bartender: "Where did you get that pig?"
Lady: "It's a duck"
Bartender: "I was talking to the duck!"

What do you call an alligator in a vest?
An investigator.

What's orange and sounds like a parrot?
A carrot.

Head lice are now resistant to usual medical treatments.
The problem has scientists scratching their heads.

What do gay horses eat?
Hhhhhhaaaaaaaaaaaaaayyyyyyyyy

What do you call a chicken staring at a lettuce?
Chicken sees a salad.

I turned into a cat earlier.
Don't ask meow!

What type of pet just lies there and does nothing.
A carpet.

A police man just knocked on my door and told me my dogs were
chasing people on bikes. I thought, it can't be my dogs
they don't even own bikes.

What do you get if you cross a pelican and a zebra?
Two streets further away.

My grandad races pigeons.
I don't know why - he never beats them.

My horse will only come out of it's stable when it gets dark.
It's becoming a night mare.

My wife told me to stop impersonating a flamingo.
I had to put my foot down.

Why wouldn't the lobster share his toys?
Because he was shellfish.

I just had to take my chameleon to the vets
as he can't change colour anymore.
He's been diagnosed with a reptile dysfunction.

Why is Pingu's dad always ironing
when none of them wear clothes?

The dog is barking at the backdoor and the wife
is yelling at the front door. Who do you let in first?
The dog, because he'll shut up when he comes in.

ANIMAL SH!T

Why can't Tommy the T-Rex clap?
Because dinosaurs have been extinct for 65 million years.

The urge to sing "The lion sleeps tonight"
is only ever a whim away.

I was walking down the road when I suddenly questioned.
Who picks up a guide dog's shit?

What do you call a parade of rabbits hopping backwards?
A receding hareline.

A lorry-load of tortoises crashed into a train-load of terrapins.
It's a turtle disaster.

I've bought a new sat nav, it's really good.
Yesterday I drove past a Zoo and it said bear left.

Such sad news to hear about the puppy that died in a washing machine.
At least it died in comfort.

What's the difference between a dirty bus stop
and a voluptuous lobster?
One's a crusty bus station and the other's a busty crustacean.

Naked man arrives at a fancy dress with a girl on his back.
"I'm a turtle" he says.
"Oh.. Who's on your back?"
"That's Michelle."

Why do squirrels swim on their backs?
To keep their nuts dry!

I used to run a dating agency for chickens.
Had to stop it though as I was struggling to make hens meet.

If Hitler was a sea creature he'd be adolfin.

I'm feeling a bit gutted, honestly thought I'd win the
giant butterfly competition. I told everyone I would win.
Me and my big moth.

People in the UK eat more bananas than monkeys.
Last year they consumed 85,736,336 bananas and only 6 monkeys!

What do you call a pond filled with fake fish?
A de-koi pond!

Somebody just threw a bottle of omega 3 capsules at me.
I only have super fish oil injuries but I'm lucky I wasn't krilled!

So I went to the dentist.
He said "Say Aaah", I said "Why?" He said
"My dog's died."

What do you call a magic dog?
A Labracadabrador.

What lies dead, a hundred feet in the air?
A dead centipede.

How do Mexicans stay warm?
They use chickens for heaters.

Capital letters.
The difference between helping your Uncle Jack off a horse
and helping your uncle jack off a horse.

What's wet and slimy and flaps about on a church floor?
A lost sole.

Why do seagulls live by the sea?
Because if they lived by the bay they'd be bagels.

Teacher: Jimmy you've spent the whole lesson drawing a pair of stoats!
Jimmy: Sorry Miss, I'm two-weaselly distracted.

Bought the wife a Pug dog.
Despite the squashed nose, bulging eyes, rolls of fat and being ugly,
the dog seems to like her!

Why are dogs such bad dancers?
Because they have two left feet.

No matter how stupid you feel, remember, Little Red Riding Hood
couldn't figure out a talking wolf in drag wasn't her grandmother.

Why did the walrus go to the Tupperware party?
He was looking for a tight seal.

Today, I'm going to open up the time capsule
I made when I was a kid.
I can't wait to see how big my puppy is now!

Need an ark to save two of every animal?
I Noah guy.

How many tickles does it take to make an octopus laugh?
Ten-tickles.

I thought that pulling the shell off my racing snail
would help it move faster.
If anything it became more sluggish.

Went for an interview at a Blacksmiths
Blacksmith: "Are you any good at shoeing horses?"
I said: "No but I once told a donkey to fuck off."

I said to this bloke "I bet there isn't a single subject
I don't have a joke about!"
He said "Beavers?"
I said "Dam!"

RSPCA have said I can't keep my pet dolphin in the bath.
Apparently it's not fit for porpoise.

My dog only responds to commands in Spanish.
He's Espanyol!

What stands in a field and goes "Oooooh!"
A cow with no lips.

What did the buffalo say to his son as he left for school?
Bison.

An insect flew into our kitchen last night,
flew around and then exploded.
I think it was a jihadi long legs.

What happened to the cow that jumped over the barbed wire fence?
Udder destruction.

I hate two types of people:
1) People who find a way of putting animals into words
when they aren't actually there.
2) Hippocrites.

My grandad had the heart of a lion
and a lifetime ban from London zoo.

A big cat escaped it's cage at the zoo yesterday.
If I saw that I'd puma pants.

I saw a man at the beach yelling. "Help, Shark!"
Somehow I knew that shark wasn't going to help him.

Where do fish keep their money?
In a riverbank.

I went to the zoo this morning only to find out that
some aquatic mammals had escaped.
It was otter chaos.

What do you call a lesbian dinosaur?
A Lickalotopus!

My mate got attacked by a grizzly in the woods the other day.
I couldn't bear to watch.

What's the difference between your girlfriend and a walrus?
One has a moustache and smells of fish
and the other is a walrus.

On which side do chickens have the most feathers?
On the outside.

Why can't Jimmy ride a bike?
Jimmy is a goldfish.

Teacher: "Name a bird with wings but can't fly?"
Student: "A dead bird, Sir."

I was in bed last night pulling my boxers off when my girlfriend
walked in and said please don't do that to the dogs!

Why do you never see elephants hiding in trees?
Because they're so good at it.

What's a duck's favourite dip?
Quackamole

Just had bubble and squeak for my dinner.
The kids didn't give a shit about those rabbits!

What's white, cold and unstable?
A bi-polar bear

My dog is named Minton.
Today he ate a shuttlecock.
Bad Minton!

My pet mouse Elvis died today.
He was caught in a trap!

What do you call a fly with no wings?
Still a fly.
The irony is unfortunate, but the name doesn't change.

What do you call a fish with no eyes?
Fsh.

What's the difference between a kangaroo and a kangaroot?
One's a marsupial, the others a Geordie stuck in a lift!

Slugs are obviously snails that have been through a divorce.

I've got a chicken proof lawn.
It's impeccable.

Unfortunately I've had to close my dating agency for chickens.
I was unable to make hens meet.

Police: "What were you thinking?"
Me: "I was told releasing birds at a wedding is romantic."
Police: "They were ostriches!"

ANIMAL SH!T

When I heard they had found a cure for dyslexia,
it was like music to my arse.

Dyslexic IT technicians wait ages for a USB,
then three come along at once.

Do three dyslexics make a riot?

Why can't dyslexics tell jokes?
They always punch up the fuckline.

I saw a dyslexic Yorkshire man the other day.
He was wearing a cat flap.

A G N B
That's bang out of order!

My dyslexia has reached a new owl.

I've finally come to accept the fact I'm dyslexic
and that I'll always be dyslexic.
A leotard can't change its spots.

Today I arrested a dyslexic robber.
He walked into a bank and said.
"Air in the hands mother stickers, this is a fuck up!"

Two dyslexics are in a kitchen, one says to the other
"Can you smell food?"
The other replies "I can't even smell my own name!"

I used to date a dyslexic girl.
I took her home and she ended up cooking my sock.

Have you heard about the chap who discovered
that he's both dyslexic and gay?
He's still in Daniel!

Old McDonald was dyslexic...
O I O I E

Grab your taco, you've pulled a dyslexic Mexican.

What do you get if you cross a dyslexic,
an insomniac, and an agnostic?
Someone who lays awake at night wondering if there really is a dog.

Went to the annual disco for the UK Dyslexic Association last night.
Was great until the DJ played YMCA and then it was fucking mayhem.

"Mum! I'm going out!"
"You're not leaving this house until you change that miniskirt!"
"Why?"
"Because I can see your balls, Richard."

I only believe in 12.5% of everything the Bible says.
Which makes me an eighth theist.

Getting older is pretty much just paying bills and finally understanding
why killers in horror flicks target teenagers.

Why do women get angry on their period?
Because they ovaryact.

Some people have difficulties sleeping...
but I can do it with my eyes closed.

What's a horrible ice-breaker?
The Titanic.

I had a goal to two lose stone by the end of the year.
Just three stone to go!

I overheard two of my friends talking about me the other day.
I said, "You disgust me."
"Yes, we did." they replied.

I'm friends with 25 letters of the alphabet.
I don't know why.

Just heard that the government is banning Roman numerals!
Well, not on my watch!

Even though I've gone bald, I still keep the comb
I've had for nearly twenty years. I just can't part with it.

There are two words in life that will open a lot of doors for people.
Push and pull.

What's green and not very heavy?
Light green.

Today I was given a box of Jamaican hair extensions....
It was dreadful.

A mysterious hole has been found in the local nudist camp wall.
The police are looking into it.

I bought a battery powered clock today.
When I got home, I noticed that they had given me the wrong one.
I thought "This is a wind up!"

RANDOM SHiT

A man died today due to his obsession of taking photos of himself next to a boiling kettle. We believe he had serious selfie steam issues.

I scared the postman today by going to the door naked.
I'm not sure what scared him more, my naked body
or the fact that I knew where he lived.

What do you call someone with no body and a nose?
Nobody knows!

My mate keeps boasting that he owns a 3 foot pack of cards.
Big deal.

Carving a boob from a tree would be pretty cool.
Wooden tit.

I hate jokes that rely on visual imagery.
I've had it right up to here with them.

Have I told you this deja vu joke before?

A huge section of tree just broke off and demolished a bank in town.
I've no idea which branch it was though.

I've just watched the Harry Potter films.
I think it's a bit unrealistic if you ask me.
I mean, a ginger kid, with two friends?

I just noticed on the bookies window it said
'Open on a Sunday 11-2'.
I'll have a tenner on that.
He was open last Sunday.

I just found out that 'Aarrgghh' is not a real word.
I can't even tell you how angry I am!

Some people have a way with words.
Others not have way.

What's ET short for?
Because he's got little legs.

I've just stolen loads of swimming pool inflatables.
I think I'd better lilo.

Here's a bit of advice for you... Advi

Guy who owns the local cinema has died.
His funeral is on Monday at 12:10, 14:20 and 18:40.

Police looking for a man who stabbed
six people with knitting needles.
He seems to be following some sort of pattern.

Phoned the ramblers club - and this bloke
just went on and on.

To the thief in the wheelchair who nicked my camouflage jacket.
You can hide but you can't run.

I worried that my addiction to helter-skelters is spiralling out of control.

I was given a leaflet the other day on anger management. I lost it.

What do you call a sleepwalking nun?
A roamin' Catholic.

I wanted to tell you all about a colour I made up...
Turns out, it was just a pigment of my imagination.

I farted in a lift earlier. It was wrong on so many levels.

One of my friends is a really stubborn hardcore raver.
She keeps trying to make me rave with her!
She just won't techno for an answer.

There's a new type of broom out, it's sweeping the nation.

How do you make holy water?
Put it in a pot and boil the hell out of it.

The energizer bunny has just been arrested on a charge of battery.

What do you call a surprised Chinese man?
Ho Lee Fuk.

You didn't hear about the three big holes in the ground?
Well, well, well.

I stayed up all night wondering where the sun went.
Then it dawned on me.

Mexican and Black jokes are the worst, because once you've
heard Juan you've heard Jamal.

America, the only country in the world who have a day
off work to celebrate a film.

Just had a nice chat with my neighbour's teenage daughter.
Turns out she's right into UFOs which is handy,
as she's getting abducted tomorrow.

There's a gang going through our town, systematically shoplifting clothes in size order.
The police believe they're still at large.

I never question myself.
Why should I start now?

Dim light bulbs or bright light bulbs?
Watts the difference.

Without a doubt, my favourite Robin Williams movie is Mrs Fire.

What do you call it when Batman skips church?
Christian Bale.

What kind of shoes do ninjas wear?
Sneakers.

Accidentally swallowed some Scrabble squares.
Going for a poo could spell trouble!

What do cheap hotels and tight pants have in common?
No ballroom.

Did you know 'emas eht yltcaxe' is exactly the same backwards?

What's the difference between a dwarf and a midget?
Very little.

There's no such thing as can't!
Unless, of course, you're cockney;
then you probably are one.

Just had a water fight in the park with a bunch of local kids.
I won! No-one's a match for me and my kettle.

Only a real genius could say these four words fast
without getting tongue tied: eye, yam, stew, peed.

What is the scariest thing to read in braille?
"Do not touch."

What's red and smells like blue paint?
Red paint.

Everybody is saying stealing is wrong.
Personally, I don't buy it.

I was kidnapped by a gang of mime artists.
They did unspeakable things to me!

I'm planning to be spontaneous.
Tomorrow.

Statistically, 132% of all people exaggerate.

You know, I've often wondered, what do people
in China call their good plates?

And for our next band, would you please welcome "The Bailiffs"
Take it away boys.

I hate it when you offer someone a sincere compliment
about their moustache, and suddenly
she's not your friend anymore.

Mary and Joseph
Now they had a stable relationship.

Autocorrect is so funny.
My mum text me "I love you" and it became
"Don't come home you're a disappointment."

I've just been house hunting.
One place had mirrors covering the walls of every room.
I thought, "I can see myself living here!"

Crime that occurs in multi-story car parks
is wrong on so many levels.

How come the pirate never learned the alphabet?
Because he kept getting lost at C!

Did you hear about the man who fell into the upholstery machine?
He's all right, now. In fact, he's fully recovered.

Today someone has stolen a rock which measures 1760 yards in length.
That must be some kind of milestone.

I can explain the first rule of Patronisation Club to you if you want,
although it's pretty complicated.

I used to be addicted to the Hokey-Cokey but I turned myself around.
And that's what it's all about!

I got home and found a burglar pressing one of my shirts.
So I punched him!
You've got to strike while the iron's hot!

I went up to the manager in Argos today.
I said, "I want to buy a watch."
"Analogue?" he said.
I said, "No mate, just a watch."

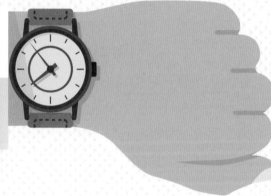

Please don't type Part A backwards.
It's a trap!

I buy all my guns from a guy called T-Rex.
He's a small arms dealer.

I've just poured superglue into a non-stick pan.
Someone's going to be wrong.

To the bloke that rudely accused me of following
his wife home last night.
I know where you live!

I don't trust stairs.
They're always up to something.

They say there's a person capable of murder
in every friendship group. I thought it was Ben,
so I killed him before he could cause any harm.

What's heavy forwards but not backwards?
A ton.

I'll tell you what I love doing more than anything...
trying to pack myself in a small suitcase!
I can hardly contain myself.

My party trick is swallowing two pieces of string and an hour later
they come out my arse tied together.
I shit you knot.

How do you get an alien baby to sleep?
Rocket.

Will I have an open casket at my funeral?
Remains to be seen.

I fell over laughing and got trapped in the trouser press.
Creased myself.

I got mugged earlier and they took my mood ring.
I really don't know how I feel about that.

FOR SALE
Broken Quiz Machine.
No questions asked.

I was at a cash machine when an old lady came up
to me and asked me to check her balance.
So I pushed her over.

Congratulations A.
Congratulations B.
Congratulations C.
It seems congratulations are in order.

I play triangle for a reggae band.
It's pretty casual.
I just stand at the back and ting.

A word of warning for you.
Beware!

I saw a midget dressed like Hitler yesterday and I thought..
"That's a little racist."

I met a girl with 12 nipples today!
Sounds fun, dozen tit.

For the first few weeks at fat club you're
normally just finding your feet.

Some guy stopped me in the street and asked
"Why are you carrying a 9ft book?" I replied... "It's a long story."

I'm in a heavy metal band.
I play lead.

Police are on the lookout for a cross-eyed burglar
They've said "If you see him peering through your window,
please warn the people next-door."

My mum said "There was someone knocking on the door, with a beard!"
I said, "No wonder I couldn't hear him!"

My annoying neighbour was banging on my door
at 3 o'clock this morning!
Luckily I was still up practising my drums.

A lot of people out there are making apocalypse jokes
like there's no tomorrow.

I went to a legless disco last night.
It was crawling with fanny.

I don't like how funerals are usually between 9-10am.
I'm not really a mourning person.

I used to think I was indecisive,
but now I'm not too sure.

You know you're ugly when it comes to a group picture
and they hand you the camera.

There are only 3 things that always tell the truth:
1 - Young Children.
2 - Drunks.
3 - Leggings.

Two reasons why I don't drink toilet water.
Number 1.
Number 2.

I know a bloke who is mute, he communicates through embroidery.
Sew to speak.

If you can't say something nice, you probably have a lisp.

Why should you never wear Ukrainian underpants?
Because Chernobyl fall out.

I gave all my dead batteries away today.
Free of charge!

How do you warm a room up that's just been painted?
Give it a second coat!

What's slippery when wet?
A wet slipper.

I remember the first time I saw a universal remote control.
I thought to myself "Well this changes everything."

My neighbour is in the book of Guinness World Records.
He's had forty four concussions! He lives very close to me.
A stone's throw away, in fact.

What's brown and sticky?
A brown stick.

I once had the honour of starting the Blackpool illuminations.
It was massive turn on.

Did you hear about these new reversible jackets?
I'm excited to see how they turn out.

I can't stand lying down.

Frozen sculptures look quite good, icy pose.

The man that invented the taser died suddenly last night.
His relatives said they were stunned.

I met this bloke with a didgeridoo and he was playing
Dancing Queen on it.
I thought, 'That's Aboriginal.'

An Indian builder has fallen through a roof
at a Lionel Richie concert!
A spokesman said "The last thing I saw was
Dan Singh on the ceiling."

I should have been sad when my torch
batteries died, but I was delighted.

How do you organise a party in space?
You planet.

Me and my mates are in a band called Duvet.
We're a cover band.

Broken puppets for sale.
No strings attached.

Two windmills are standing in a field and one asks the other,
"What kind of music do you like?"
The other says, "I'm a big metal fan"

If towels could tell jokes they would probably
have a dry sense of humour.

Just bought a suit made from cactus.
I look pretty sharp in it.

I heard the funniest time travel joke tomorrow.

Isn't it odd that the the human mind doesn't register
the the fact that "the" was used twice each time in this sentence?

RANDOM SH!T

Did you hear about the guy who bought a sponge door?
Can't knock it.

If it wasn't for blinds...
It would be curtains for us all.

A funeral was held today for the inventor of air conditioning.
Thousands of fans attended.

Man jumps in a taxi says "King Arthur's Close"
Taxi driver says "Don't worry, I'll lose him at the lights."

Yesterday a clown held a door open for me,
I thought it was a nice Jester.

Mexican friends?
I have Juan or two.

A boat carrying red paint has crashed into a boat carrying blue paint.
The crew have been marooned.

A British prisoner has squeezed four smuggled
mobile phones out of his arse.
All chargers have been dropped.

I've just won eight straight games of rock, paper, scissors against that very predictable Edward Scissorhands.

Why did the joke about the roof get no laughs?
It went over their heads.

Paddy heard that most accidents happen within two miles of home.
So he moved.

Atheism is a non-prophet organization.

Lazy People Fact #5626728943
You were too lazy to read that number.

How much did it cost the pirate to get his ears pierced?
A buck an ear.

It's really difficult to find what you want on eBay.
I was searching for cigarette lighters
but found over 15,000 matches.

There was a prison break and I saw a midget climb the fence.
As he jumped down he sneered at me and I thought,
well that's a little condescending.

I've just written a book about basements.
My publisher reckons it could be a best cellar!

How many Spaniards does it take to change a lightbulb?
Juan.

What did the cracked teacup say?
I've been mugged.

Over 90% of people over 60 believe that we show
less respect to others than we did in the past.
Silly old fuckers!

My neighbour has at last forgiven me for flashing my bum at her.
She's over the moon!

What do you say to a man who's just stolen your gate?
Nothing. He might take a fence.

I don't trust trees, they're shady.

Did you hear about the man who fell asleep at the wheel?
There was a terrible mess.
Clay everywhere.

When a women says "We need to talk"
Why is it never about football?

Why did the blind woman fall down the well?
Because she couldn't see that well.

If you're lonely, dim the lights and put on a horror movie.
After a while you won't feel like you're alone anymore.

My best mate just fainted on the London eye.
But it's okay, he's slowly coming around.

Went to the corner shop earlier.
Bought four corners.

I just bought a new blindfold,
can't see myself wearing it though.

Why is the winner of the Miss Universe contest always from earth?

Never get behind the Devil in a Post Office queue,
for the Devil has many forms.

The generation who claimed the older generation ruined their
future by voting Brexit are the generation currently
chasing imaginary Pokemon.

So, I hear reincarnation is making a comeback.

I felt like I was on The Voice today!
I farted on the bus and four people turned around!

What does a clock do when it's hungry?
It goes back four seconds.

Why are mountains so funny?
Because they're hill areas.

A bishop walks straight up to the bar and the barman says,
"You can't do that, Bishops can only move diagonally."

If you're 10% Polish, does that make you a tad pole?

Check this one out: 1

I really love my fanbase.
Without it, my fan would fall over.

They all laughed when I said I wanted to
create a funny shit joke book.
Well, they're not laughing now!